Famous & Fun Rock

11 Appealing Piano Arrangements

Carol Matz

Famous & Fun Rock, Book 2, contains 11 carefully selected popular rock hits. Each piece has been arranged especially for early elementary to elementary pianists, yet remains faithful to the sound of the original. The arrangements can be used as a supplement to any method. No eighth notes or dotted-quarter rhythms are used. The optional duet parts for teacher or parent add to the fun!

Carol Matz

Alfred

Produced by
Alfred Music
P.O. Box 10003
Van Nuys, CA 91410-0003
alfred.com

ISBN-10: 0-7390-9604-4
ISBN-13: 978-0-7390-9604-8

Splish Splash

Words and Music by
Bobby Darin and Jean Murray
Arranged by Carol Matz

Quickly

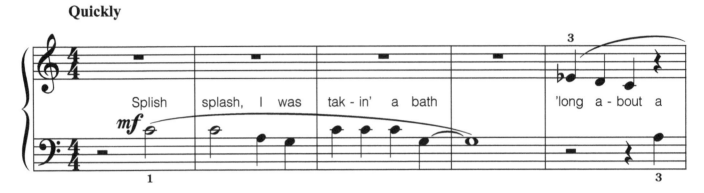

DUET PART (Student plays one octave higher)

Quickly, in two

Sat - ur - day night. A rub dub, just re - lax - in' in the

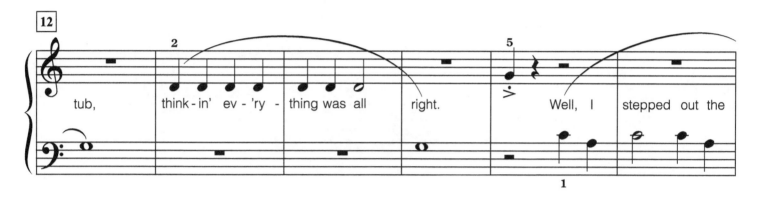

tub, think - in' ev - 'ry - thing was all right. Well, I stepped out the

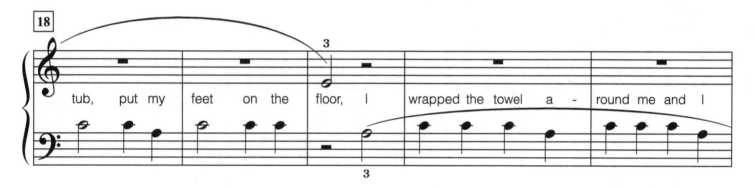

tub, put my feet on the floor, I wrapped the towel a - round me and I

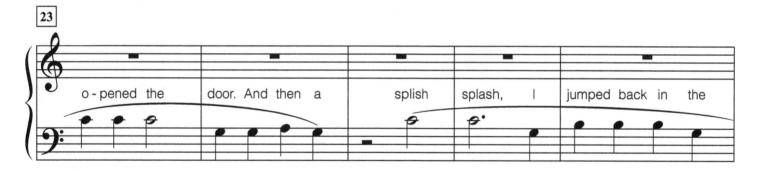

o - pened the door. And then a splish splash, I jumped back in the

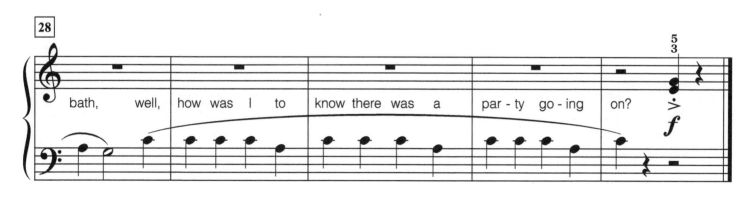

bath, well, how was I to know there was a par - ty go - ing on?

Blowin' in the Wind

Words and Music by Bob Dylan
Arranged by Carol Matz

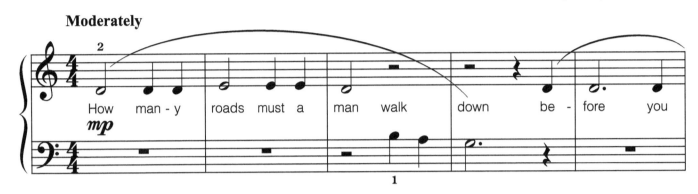

How man - y roads must a man walk down be - fore you

DUET PART (Student plays one octave higher)

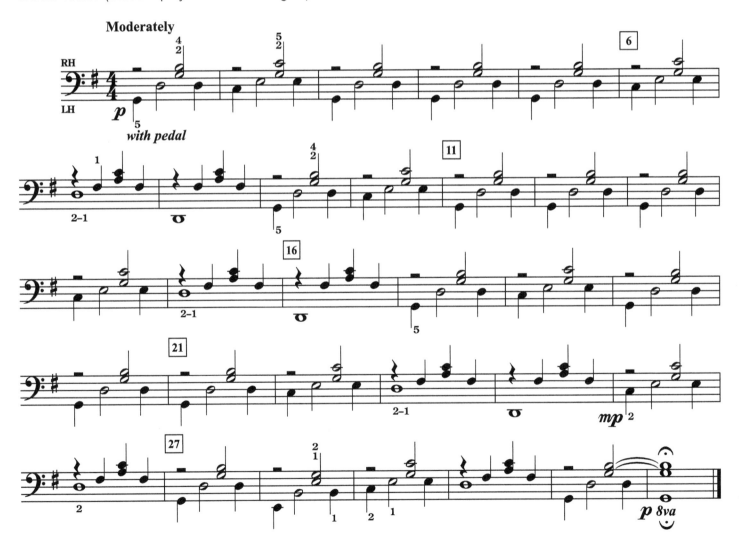

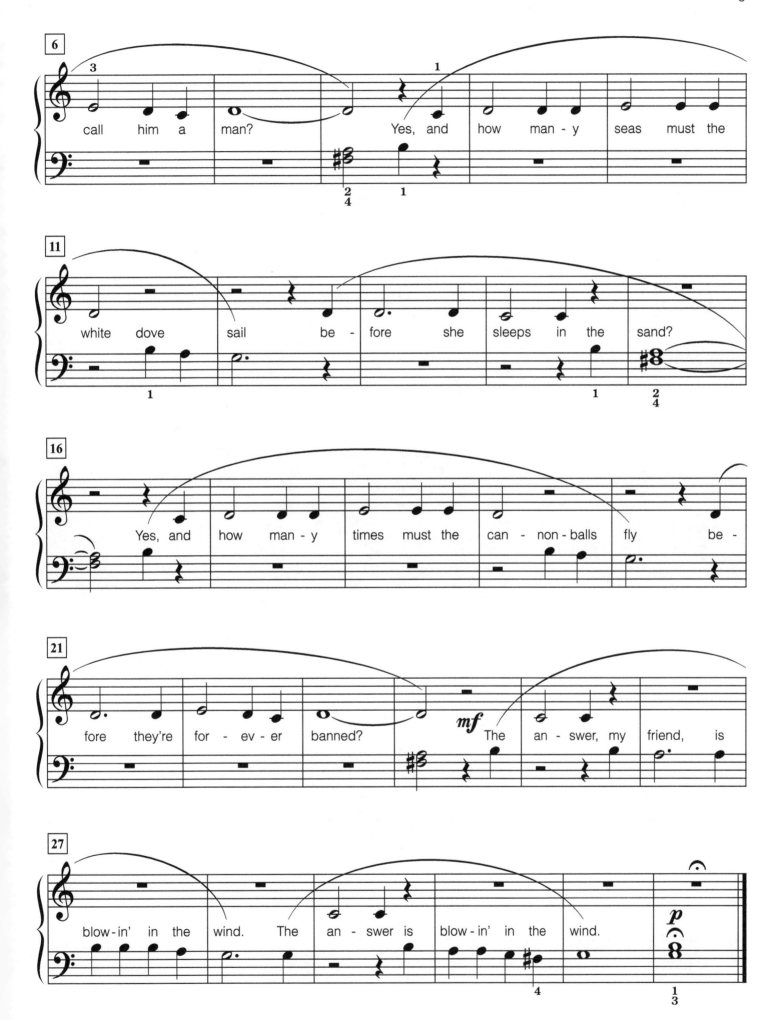

The Only Exception

Words and Music by
Hayley Williams and Josh Farro
Arranged by Carol Matz

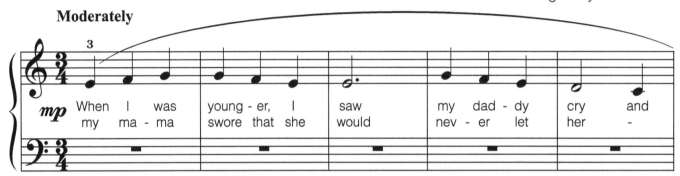

Lyrics under staff:
When I was | young - er, I | saw | my dad - dy | cry and
my ma - ma | swore that she | would | nev - er let | her -

DUET PART (Student plays one octave higher)

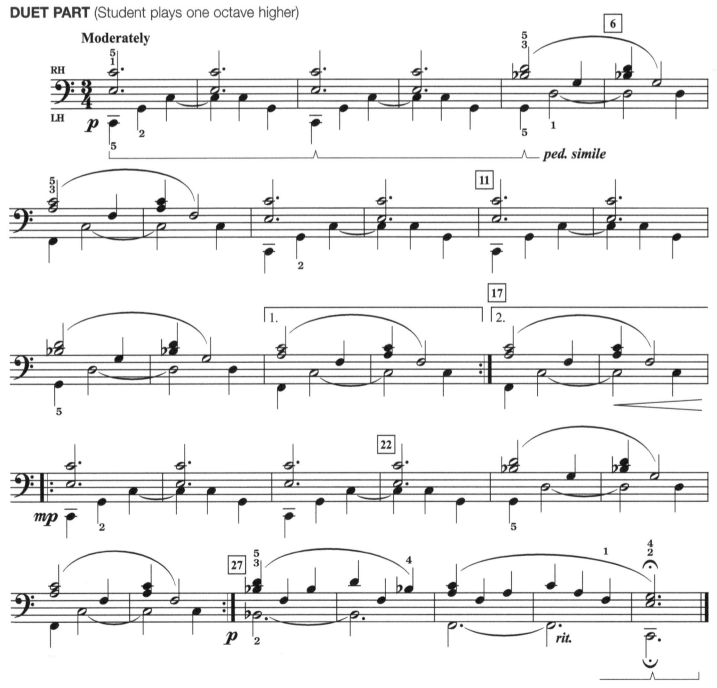

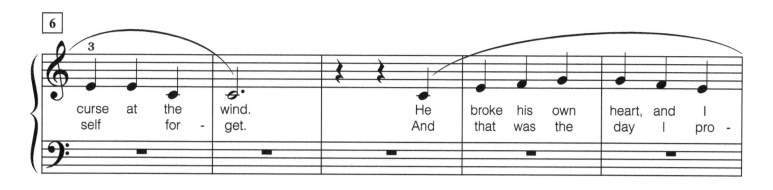

curse at the wind.
self for - get.
He
And
broke his own
that was the
heart, and I
day I pro -

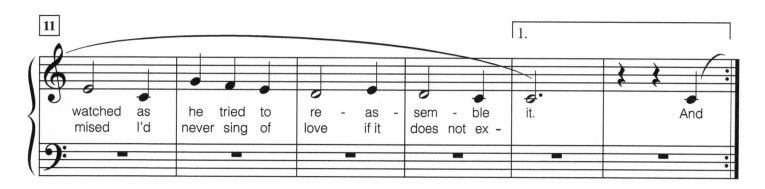

watched as he tried to re - as - sem - ble it.
mised I'd never sing of love if it does not ex -
And

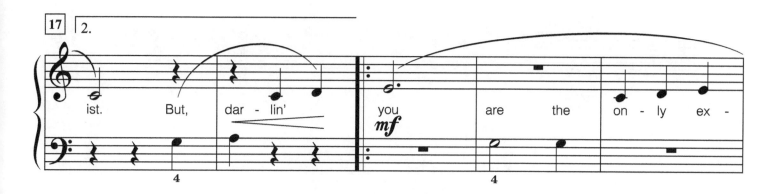

ist. But, dar - lin' you are the on - ly ex -
mf

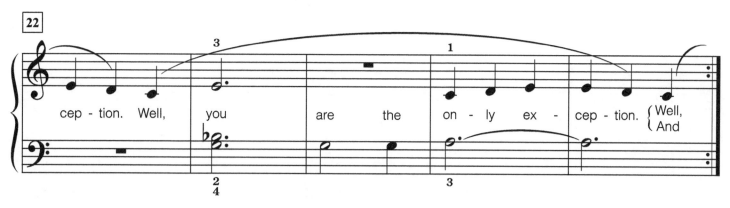

cep - tion. Well, you are the on - ly ex - cep - tion. { Well,
{ And

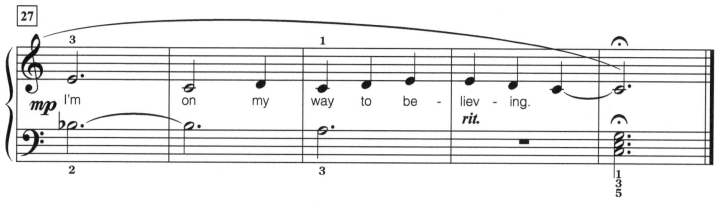

mp I'm on my way to be - liev - ing.
rit.

Itsy Bitsy Teenie Weenie Yellow Polka Dot Bikini

Words and Music by
Paul J. Vance and Lee Pockriss
Arranged by Carol Matz

Moderately fast

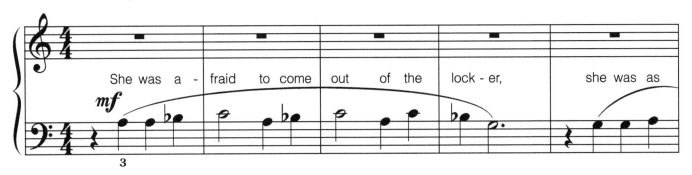

She was a - fraid to come out of the lock - er, she was as

DUET PART (Student plays one octave higher)

Moderately fast, in two

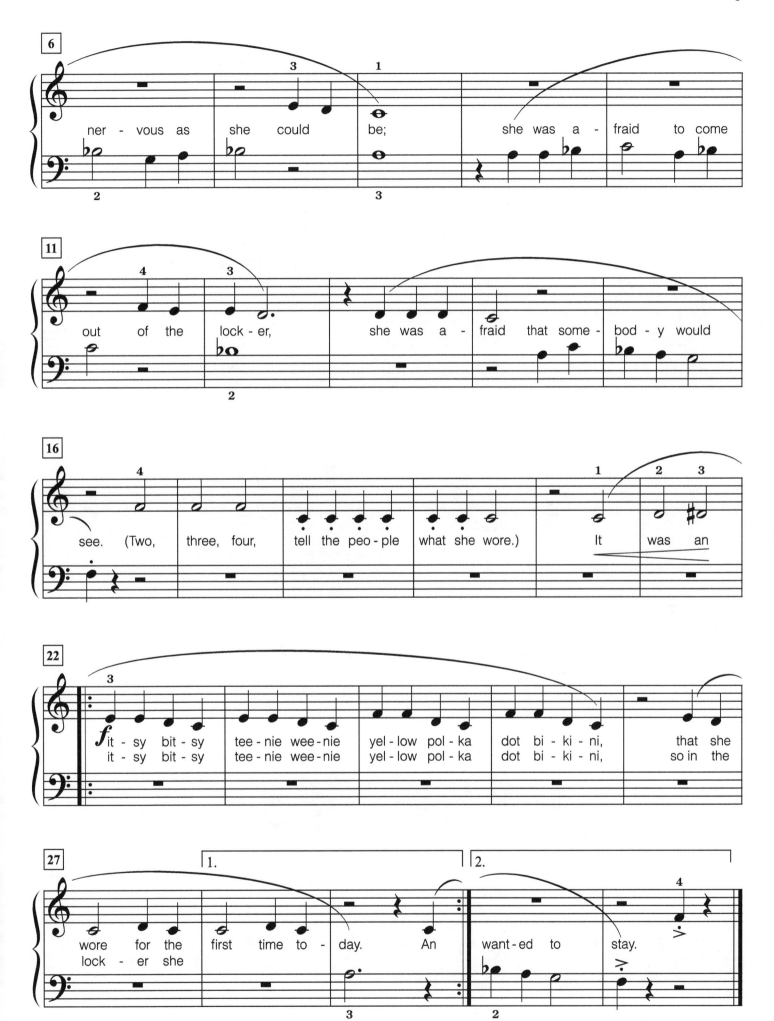

Boulevard of Broken Dreams

Lyrics by Billie Joe
Music by Green Day
Arranged by Carol Matz

Moderately

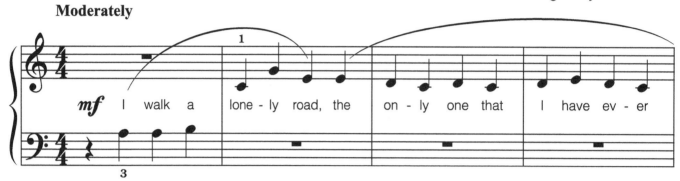

I walk a lone-ly road, the on-ly one that I have ev-er

DUET PART (Student plays one octave higher)

Moderately

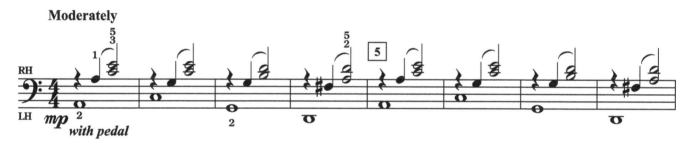

Hey There Delilah

Words and Music by Tom Higgenson
Arranged by Carol Matz

Quickly

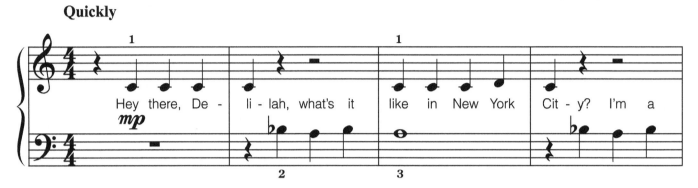

Hey there, De - li - lah, what's it like in New York Cit - y? I'm a

DUET PART (Student plays one octave higher)

Quickly, in two

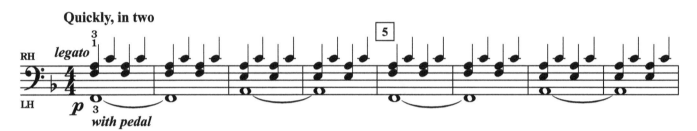

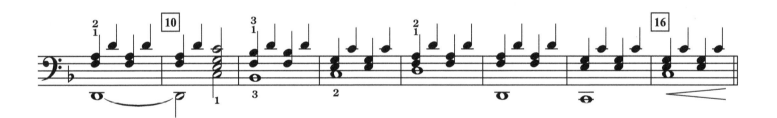

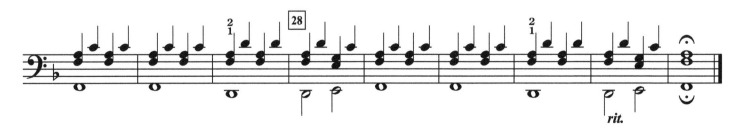

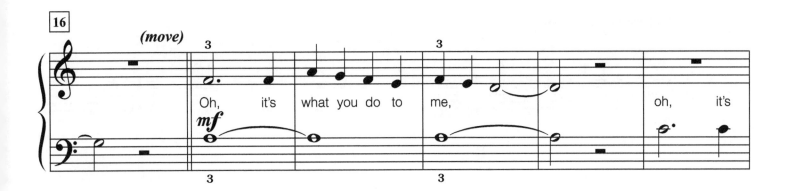

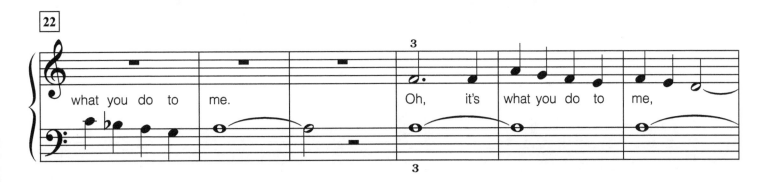

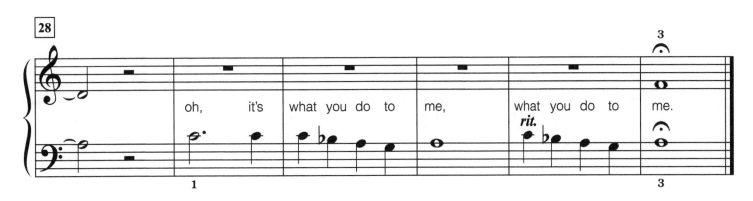

All I Have to Do Is Dream

Words and Music by Boudleaux Bryant
Arranged by Carol Matz

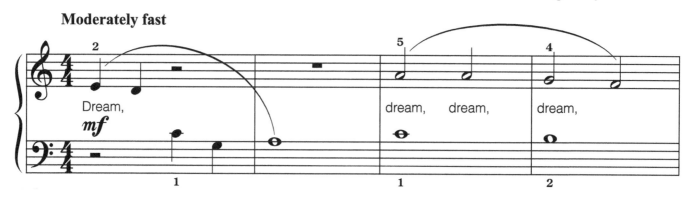

DUET PART (Student plays one octave higher)

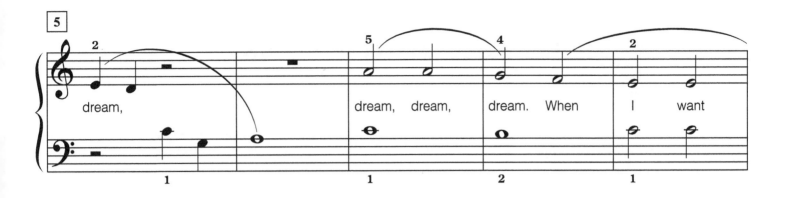

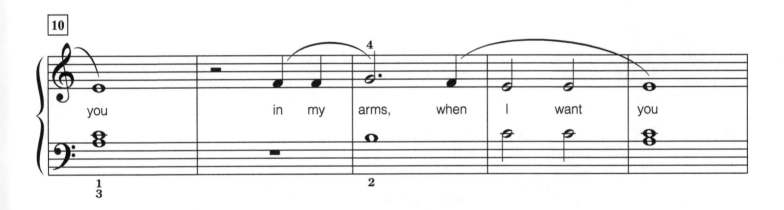

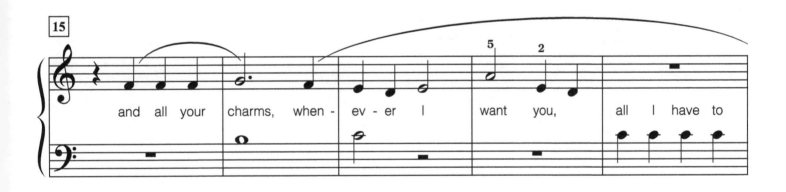

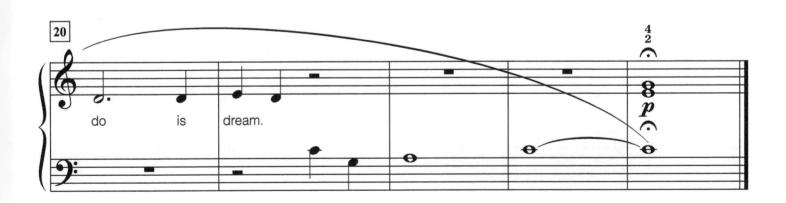

Mr. Tambourine Man

Words and Music by Bob Dylan
Arranged by Carol Matz

DUET PART (Student plays one octave higher)

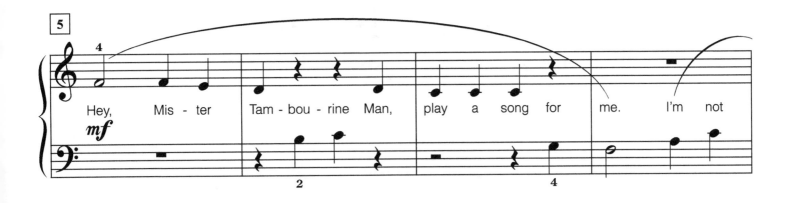

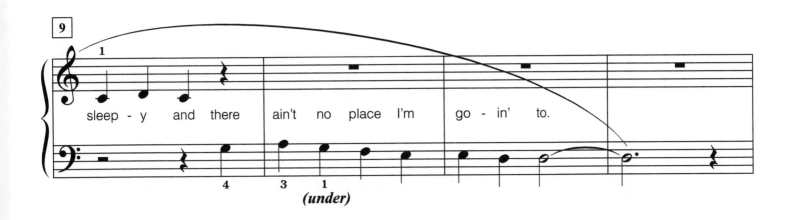

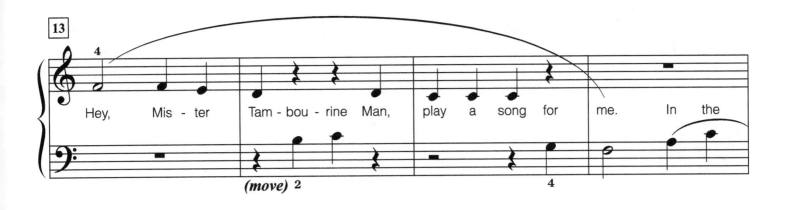

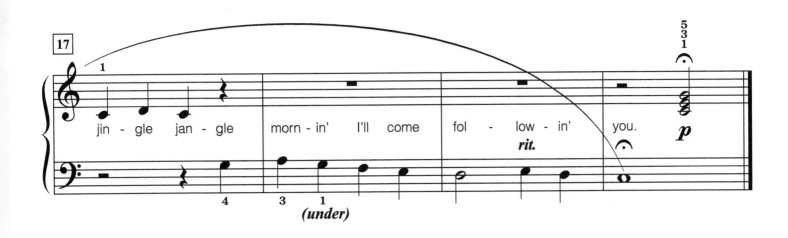

Good Riddance
(Time of Your Life)

Lyrics by Billie Joe
Music by Green Day
Arranged by Carol Matz

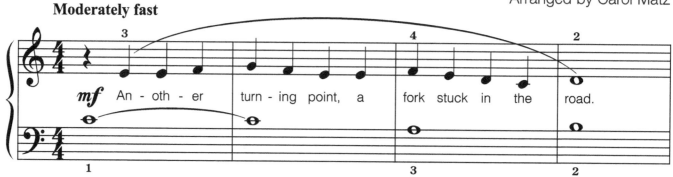

An - oth - er turn - ing point, a fork stuck in the road.

DUET PART (Student plays one octave higher)

19

Wipe Out

By The Surfaris
Arranged by Carol Matz

Quickly

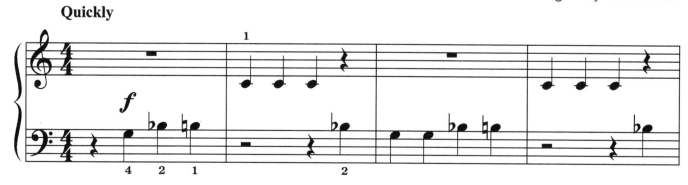

DUET PART (Student plays one octave higher)

Quickly, in two

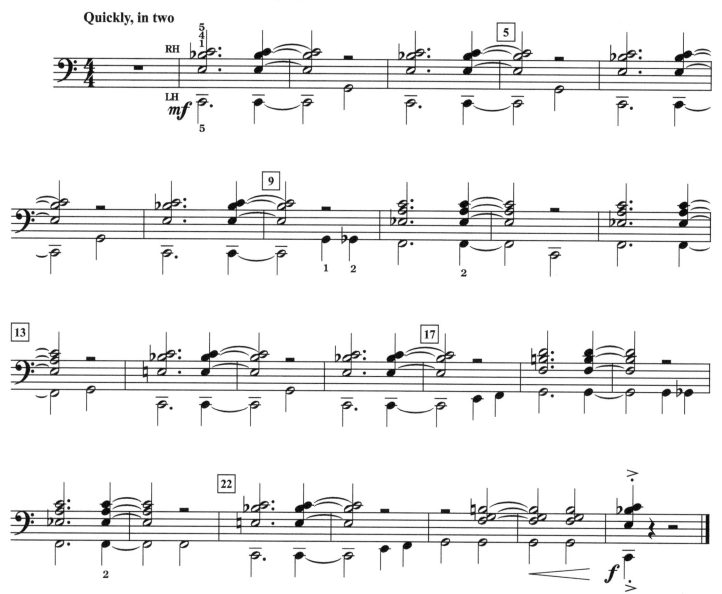

Eye of the Tiger

Words and Music by
Frankie Sullivan III and Jim Peterik
Arranged by Carol Matz

Moderately fast

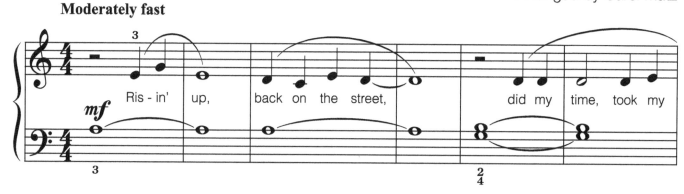

DUET PART (Student plays one octave higher)

Moderately fast, in two